The Kiwi Branding Edge

Buy New Zealand Made

Cover Image: Gary Horne, centralstation.co.nz

Authored by Ryan L. Jennings

Edited by Dane Ambler

Photography by Anna Heyward

Publisher: Umprint Publishing umprint.net
100% Kiwi Business book also available

ISBN 978-0-473-49416-2

140p 1.8cm

All photos unless otherwise attributed by Anna Heyward
aheyward@buynz.org.nz.

A catalogue record for this book is available from the National Library
of New Zealand.

The Kiwi Branding Edge

for Business Owners, Marketers and Exporters

Buy New Zealand Made

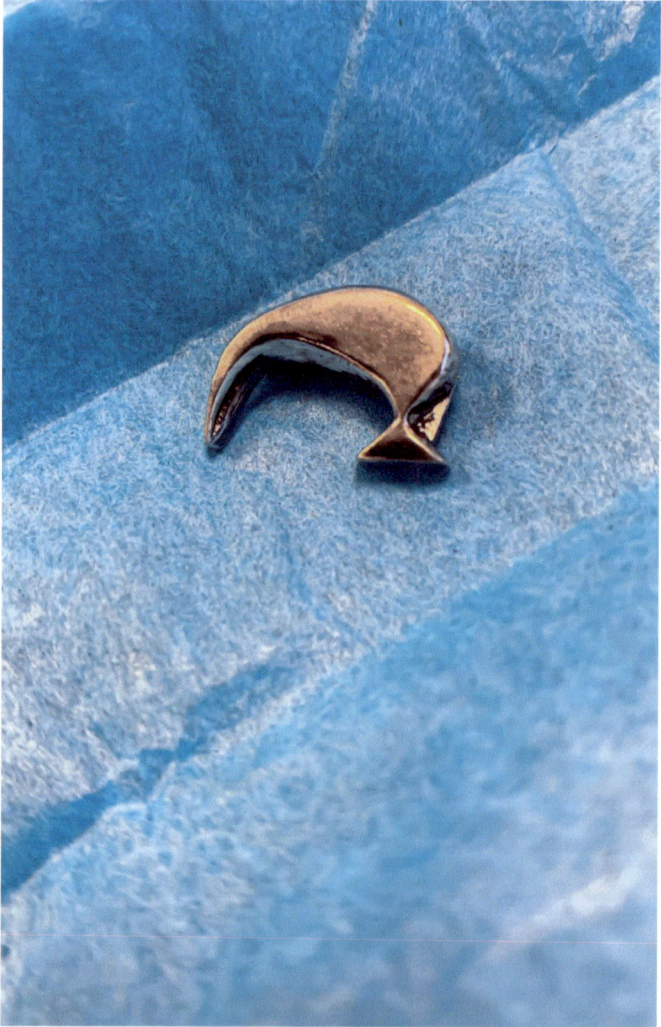

Handcrafted by Lara Hopwood at Geo Jewellery

Author's Note

A quality product was sufficient to compete in the 20th century.

Now industrialisation has combined with globalisation to render quality a commodity in many product categories.

That creates is a business opportunity for you.

An opportunity to go beyond commoditised quality.

An opportunity to pick two edges, that when combined are valued by the few not the many.

An opportunity to make something remarkable.

That the few remark on and tell the others for you.

Consumers want to play on the edges.

Smart manufacturers are intentional about what edges they create.

Go Beyond Quality

What might this mean?

A high-quality New Zealand Made product combined with thoughtful packaging is an edge with the newly-minted middle class in Asia who trust what New Zealand makes.

A high-quality New Zealand Made product that doesn't hurt the environment or the people who make it is an edge that will get you adoration with the next generation of consumers.

A New Zealand Made product that weaves in the Kiwi story is an edge that might just keep customers from switching to a vanilla competitor that produces more for less.

Edge Is Everything

Going beyond quality means being intentional about who your product is for.

The Kiwi trademark must create an advantage for you in the eyes of who your product is for.

New Zealand Made is not for businesses that don't want to create a market origin advantage through country of origin labelling.

This book is a branding guide that shares the business edges that are working for Kiwi companies.

Use this guide as inspiration and create your edges with confidence.

Ryan Jennings
@businesskiwi
Executive Director - Buy New Zealand Made

New Zealand Made. Logo Or Brand?

The New Zealand Kiwi trademark is a label, a sticker, a logo and a brand.

'New Zealand Made' says something about the product or service it is added to, and as a marketer, there is more than one way to go about adding it to what you do.

Branding should go beyond what looks right. It should share a deeper message.

A branded product or service consists of two parts. The first is *required* and the second *desired*. Without both, there is no brand… it's just a logo.

The first is that someone who isn't even using the product, can tell from a distance that it was made in New Zealand. It should appear that it could only be made by you the maker... the manufacturer.

If the customer or casual observer can't tell who made it, then there is no brand.

That's the distinction between a generic logo and a specific brand.

The second is the desire to be noticed. Successfully branded items succeed because the owner enjoys that the brand is noticed in daily use, either by others or even by themselves.

Photo: Aotearoa Nutrients

"Our customers trust products with the New Zealand Made logo on it. It's an essential component in confirming the authenticity of where they are produced and manufactured.

"We are extremely proud of this and the New Zealand Made logo helps represent all of what our products stand for."

Warren Hignett, General Manager, Aotearoa Nutrients.

Te Puna Coasters made from Paulownia timber

Table Of Contents

QUICK START GUIDE

There are ten ways to benefit as a licence holder of the New Zealand Made Kiwi trademark.

1. Frame Your Certificate

2. Label Your Products

3. Add The Website Widget

4. Label Your Printed Collateral

5. Label Your Packaging

6. Send Us What You've Made

7. Ask Us To Film What You Make

8. Send Your Hero Video

9. See How Kiwi Businesses Are Growing

10. Business Consulting

Check to see what products you're eligible to apply the Kiwi trademark to at buynz.org.nz.

To apply the Kiwi trademark, you must be an Official New Zealand Made Licence Holder.

Photo: Lore

Leverage The Kiwi Trademark

This guide illustrates best practice in integrating the Kiwi trademark with your brand in a way that speaks to where you're going, so those who want to follow can pick up on your signal.

We'll show you what exemplar use looks like and what's working for Kiwi businesses.

Flick through this book, get inspired and then decide which provenance marketing strategy is going to work for you.

Pictured: Chantal Gellert holding the Certificate of Licence for RocketSpark

1. Frame Your Certificate

Your Certificate of Licence deserves to be framed and hung on the wall.

Show your customers, employees and suppliers that you are an Official New Zealand Made Licence Holder.

Your Licence Number is unique to you and should be shown at your place of work and on your website.

You'll automatically receive a new Certificate of Licence every year in July upon payment of your annual licence fee.

Photo: Weebits

2. Add The Logo
To Your Products

Chapters one to five are examples of how Kiwi businesses are labelling their products.

Be inspired by the amazing, powerful and beautiful ways that the logo has been added by over 1,200 Kiwi businesses who manufacturer and make in New Zealand.

Hint: The most popular choice is the 25mm black and white primary logo.

Of course, decide what's going to work best for you and your business.

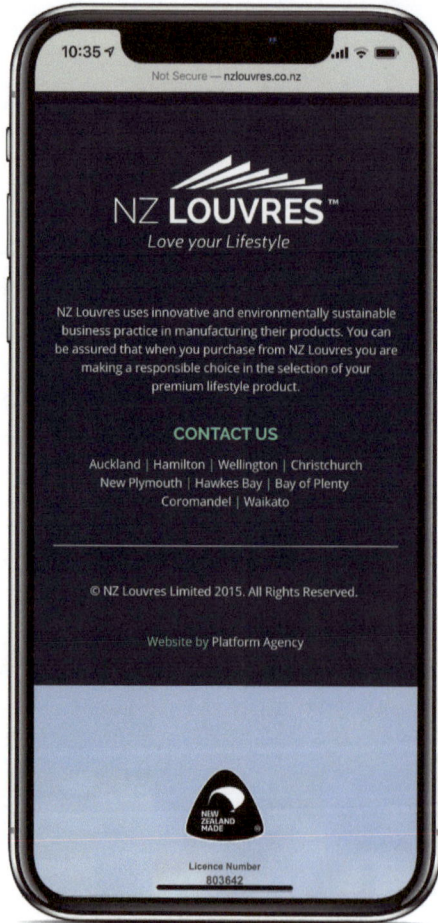

3. Add The Logo To Your Website

The website widget is a few lines of code to display your licence number next to the New Zealand Made logo in the footer of your website.

It even automatically links to your list of licensed products on our website buynz.org.nz.

This is placed on the bottom of your website footer when the majority of the products displayed on your website are New Zealand Made.

When only a few products or a single product is manufactured in New Zealand, the website widget is placed on the product category page or the product page.

NZ Louvres make roof systems for Kiwi homes. Potential buyers care about where a product is made, so by displaying their website widget it creates a market origin advantage for NZ Louvres.

"The decision to manufacture right here in New Zealand, where we can ensure the best componentry, innovation in design and do our bit for the environment we love, is an easy one." Steffan Haua, Director.

When a visitor taps on the NZ Made logo on *nzlouvres.co.nz*, it takes the visitor through to a licensed product list on *buynz.org.nz/803642* helping verify the roof systems as New Zealand Made.

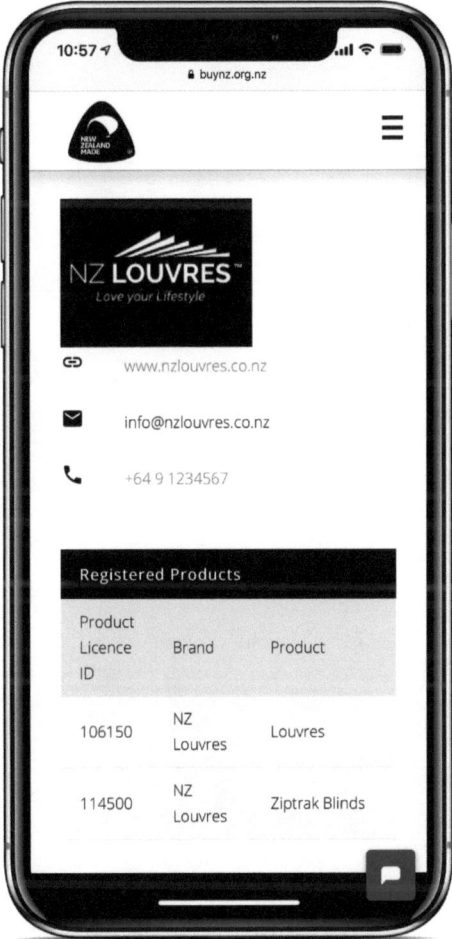

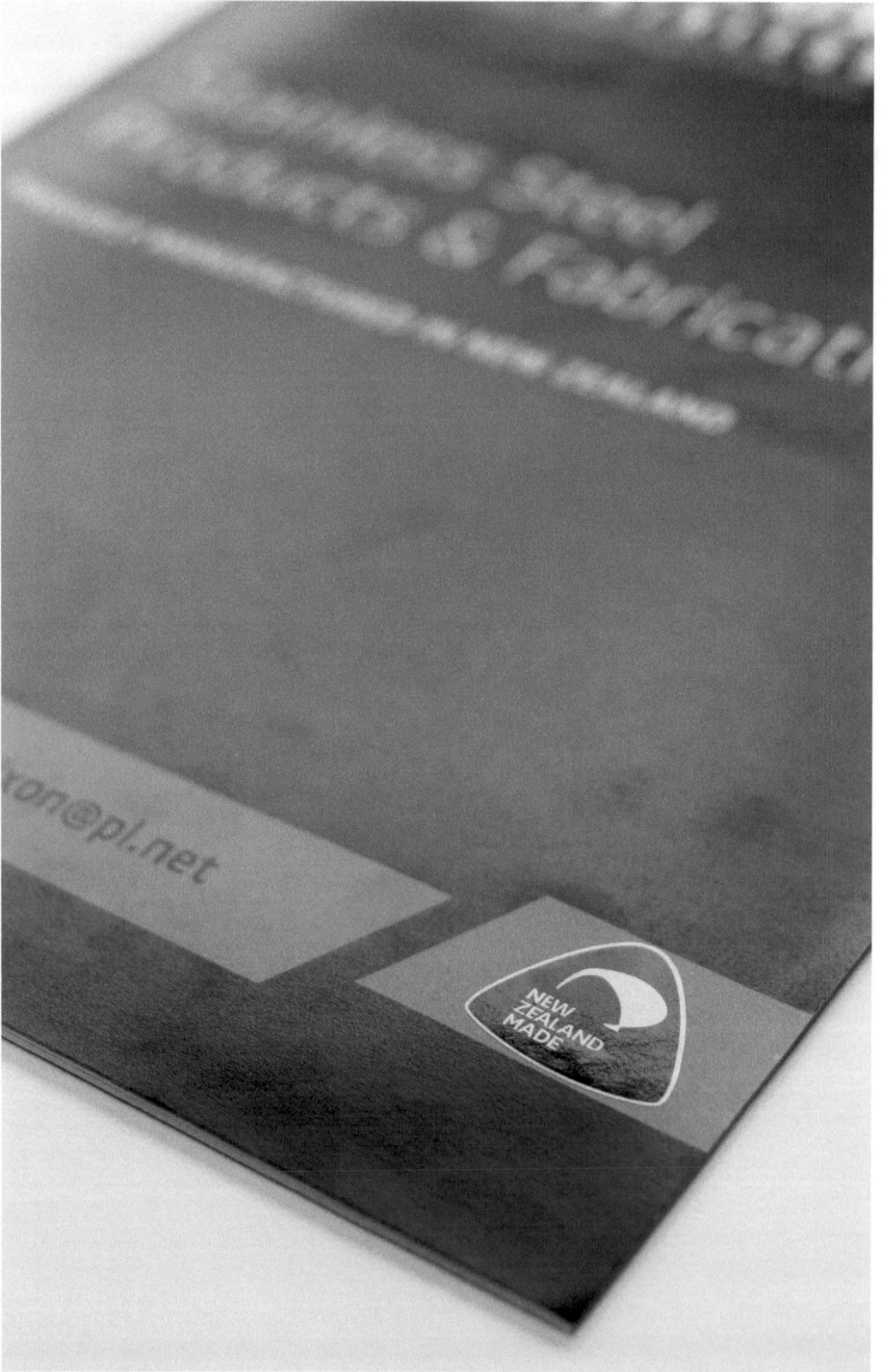

Dixon Manufacturing

4. Add The Logo To Printed Marketing Collateral

Printed catalogues are an excellent place to add the Kiwi trademark next to the products you want to highlight as New Zealand Made.

Where you rely on printed flyers or brochures, these can also be smart places to add the logo as a mark of trust and authenticity.

Aotearoa Nutrients

5. Add The Logo To Your Packaging

Packaging is another opportunity to add the Kiwi trademark alongside your company name so that every person who handles your product along the supply chain knows this product is New Zealand Made.

Aotearoa Nutrients Limited has taken their own colour palette and integrated it into the logo for the infant formula they produce for domestic and export consumption.

Provenance Marketing
Show Featured Businesses

Lightstudio, Cable Camel, PakWorld, KiwiHerb, Fresh Haircare, Rock-It Board, Rainbow Confectionery, Vista Drinks, WhatMakesNZ, Independent Lens Specialists, Little Paper Hugs, Native Woodcraft, Mossops Honey, National Candles, Aspiring Safety, Trailer World, The Furnace, Damba Chairs, Parisian Neckwear, Ouchie Powder, Animal Health Direct, Te Puna, Sewphist, Summer Rose Cottage, Dry Cuffs, Wild Country Foods, Nil Products, simplenakedsoap, Odorex, Healthpak, Skinny Fizz, Cactus Outdoor, Earth Sea Sky, Dept. of Soul, Wilson Consumer Products, Newflands, Savvy Touch, Ultimate Feeds, House of Baddeck, Cosy Toes, Sugoi Publishing, Herbology, Oku, Complete Kids Nutrition, Aotearoa Nutrients, Nom Global, Bluebird, PopNGood, ETA, RJ's Licorice, Mayceys Confectionery, Griffins, The Hemp Store, Paua World, The Good Use Company, Carousel Confectionery, NZ Gold Health, Dixon Manufacturing, HoneyWrap, Talula Tween Wear, Nature's Beauty.

6. Send Us What You've Made

Once you've ordered labels and downloaded your artwork, label your products and send us what you've made.

We'll feature your product on The Provenance Marketing Show like the 61 businesses shown on the opposite page.

Watch The Provenance Marketing Show on youtube.com/buynzmade.

Making It New Zealand Featured Businesses

Robax Products, Morrifield Tunnelhouses, Southern Fresh Produce, Hills Hats, Taurus Leather, National Candles, Cibocal Cutting Boards, Jens Hansen Jewellers, Talley's Ice Cream, Goldpine, Earth Sea Sky, Fielden Metalworks, Oasis Beauty, NZ Sock Company, Independent Lens Specialists, Phytomed, House of Baddeck, HELLA, Felton, Rainbow Confectionery, Van Lier Nurseries, WMC Trail Tools, EPI Plastics, Whitestone Cheese, Sutton Tools, Harraways, The Copy Press, Seventhwave Wetsuits, simplenakedsoap, Dairy Nutraceuticals, Weebits, Goldfields Print & Packaging, Trailer World, Powerglide Elevators, Rock-It Board, McKinlays Footwear, CS For Doors, Dynamic Inspection, Hansells Masterton, T&R Interior Systems, Aerofast and Stanley Innovations.

Simon Berry, Whitestone Cheese

7. Invite Us To Film What You Make

The 'Making It New Zealand' series uncovers what Kiwis are making in New Zealand.

Each episode is optimised for social newsfeeds. We film, edit and run the entire marketing campaign for you, like the 42 businesses shown on the opposite page. Watch the Making It New Zealand Series on youtube.com/buynzmade.

"The Making it New Zealand Series helped us to share our story by creating a behind the scenes digital message. This provided a fantastic window on our operation. Having your company's story told from a 3rd person perspective adds fantastic PR value." Simon Berry, Managing Director Whitestone Cheese.

Gabrielle Simpson, NZ Sock Co.

8. Send Us Your Hero Video

We'll make a 60 second social media commercial and create a marketing campaign from it.

You get to decide:

1. The marketing goal and where you want customers to go next.

2. Your product page to promote.

3. Your service to book.

4. Your phone to call.

"Manufacturing in New Zealand helps our 3rd generation family business foster growth, not only in our industry, but that of our community and it provides a future of job security for many people.

"It gives us a sense of pride to be able to offer the world a high-quality technical product that's made right here in New Zealand."

Gabrielle Simpson, International Sales, Manager NZ Sock Co.

This product has been made to
Griffin's highest quality standards.
r comments and compliments
e call Customer Services on
74 334 (0800 GRIFFINS)
1800 725 940 (Aust).

NEW
ZEALAND
MADE

Made in New Zealand

Store in a cool,
dry place. Once
opened, place
in an airtight
container.

PLEASE
DISPOSE OF
PACKAGING
CAREFULLY

PEANUTS AND TREE NUTS.

GRAINES DE SÉSAME
FABRIQUÉ DANS U
ARACHIDES ET N

9. See How Kiwi Businesses Are Growing

You're one of many New Zealand makers and manufacturers who add the Kiwi trademark to what they do.

Learn from others and we'll all improve faster.

Follow at:

Youtube.com/buynzmade

Instagram.com/buynzmade

Facebook.com/buynzmadecampaign

Ryan Jennings, Executive Director
Buy New Zealand Made

10. Arrange A 20 Minute Call

Our Executive Director Ryan Jennings likes to speak with people in New Zealand who are making business happen. Request a 20 minute call.

Each call is pre-arranged and recorded, so this is an opportunity to talk about what you do and get a more nuanced answer on how to apply what we do to what you do.

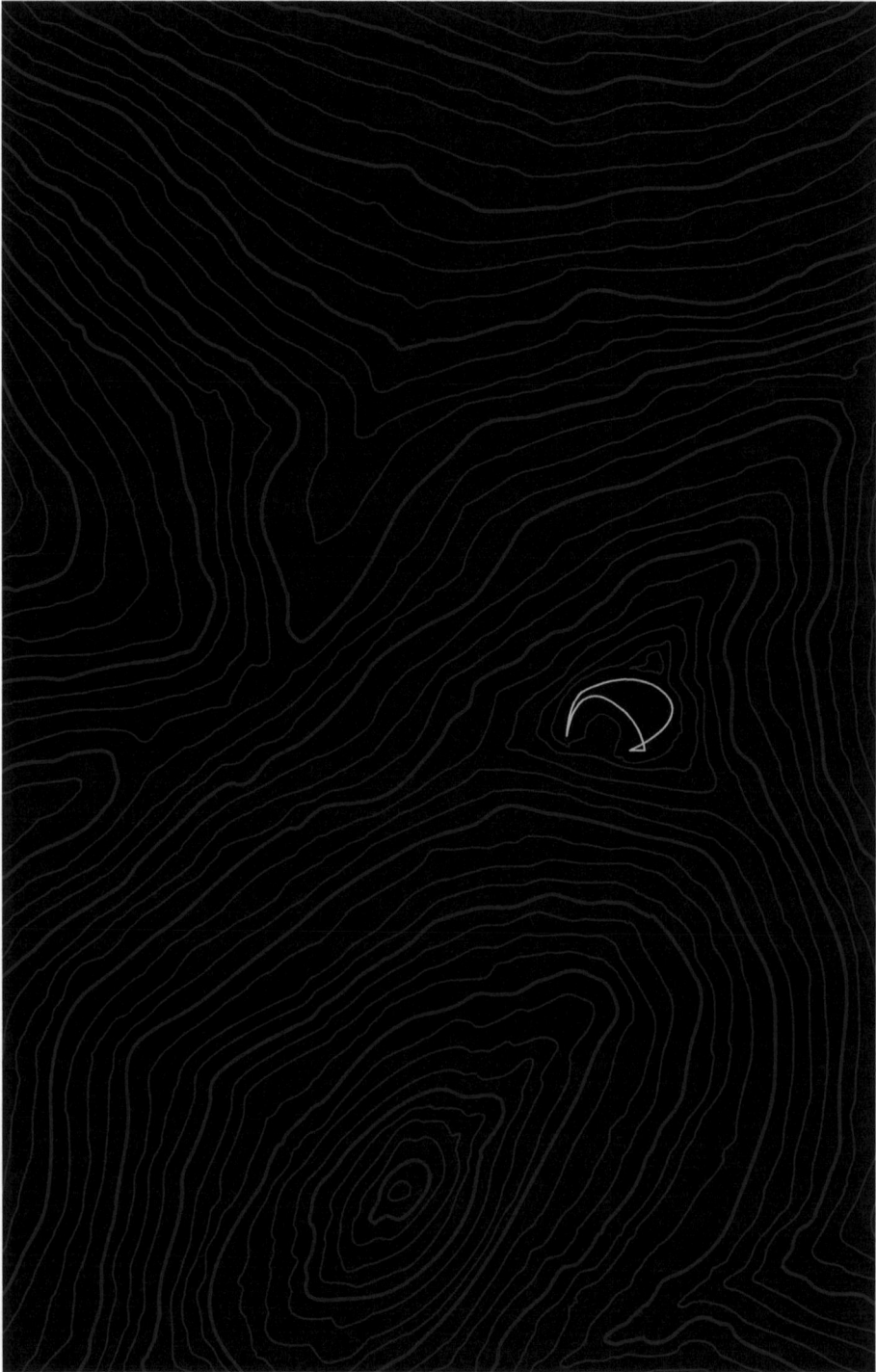

Design: Gary Horne, Central Station

CHAPTER ONE

Primary Logo
Applications

Our primary logo is in black and white
and is found on the majority of licensed
products labelled as New Zealand Made.

This chapter looks at the primary ways of
applying the Kiwi trademark to what you do
through the lens of those who are already having
success with their country of origin solutions.

Jewel Sized Labels

10mm label

Natty is the brainchild of Cat Mckay who makes her jewellery at her design studio in Berhampore, Wellington.

These include items such as the mānuka earrings and necklaces, and huia feather and kererū brooches shown.

Photo: Natty

"Natty creates beautiful mementos, without being overtly 'kiwi'. Each design is composed of rimu, decorated with vibrant patterns and designs and hand-painted in house, inspired by the beauty and nature of Aotearoa." Founder, Cat Mc Kay says.

Her products are available directly from her studio, at ifeelnatty.com or from one of over 100 stockists throughout New Zealand.

Paua World applies the 10mm label on their range of jewellery such as this New Zealand paua shell encased in 22k gold plated jewellery. The Kiwi logo serves as a mark of provenance for Paua World.

Paua World jewellery made from paua.

Little Paper Hugs is bringing back the thrill of finding a card, letter or gift in the mailbox that says someone is thinking of you.

Every card is printed with the New Zealand Made Kiwi logo on the reverse.

Ativa Dichroic Glass is a combination of individually hand-cut, shaped and layered art glass which is then fused with metal oxide dichroic compounds.

"All our pieces are proudly designed and handcrafted in New Zealand, making each piece truly unique." Logan Belworthy, Ativa Jewellery.

Refillable Retail Products Labelled

25mm label

Kahuku Natural make products almost entirely from plant-based products. Their edge is what their products exclude. No palm oils, no animal products, no preservatives, no synthetics and no chemicals.

Kahuku's world-first refill program delivers stainless steel product dispensers to retail stores instead of plastic and retailers are on getting on board.

"Kahuku Naturals has proved that a product refill system is achievable and we can change the way we consume. Bulk filling products cuts back on personal packaging waste but is fruitless if the bulk containers are being dropped straight into landfill.

To move forward to a sustainable future we need to look outside current systems and models and re-create how we can consume." Vicki Bailey, Kahuku Natural.

That is a New Zealand made product story worth sharing.

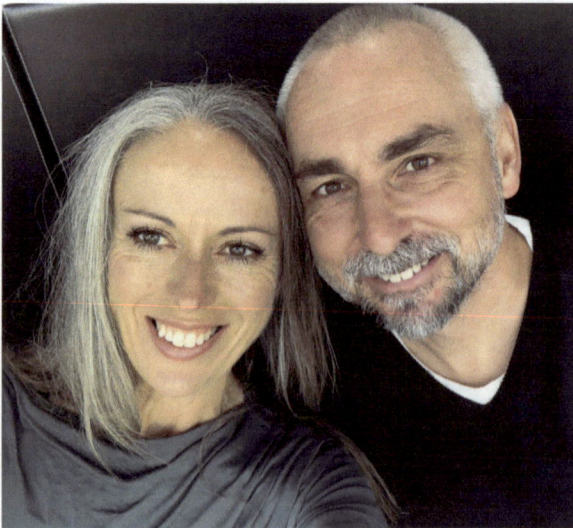

Photo: Vicki and Andrew Bailey

Photo: Kahuku Natural

It's Hip To Be Rectanglar

36mm rectangle

Not all products are going to suit the iconic rounded triangle edges of the logo and that's o.k. by us. When you want your provenance marketing to remain in keeping with your products' angular design, consider the modern rectangle label.

Author Joanna Hamilton applies this label on the front left of the books she publishes via Sugoi Publishing with her stamp applied in the bottom right of her published book.

Packs Of Reusability

Nil Products create jobs for people who find it difficult
to obtain part-time work from home. To date they've
made over 500,000 beeswax wraps saving the planet from 500,000
units of plastic rubbish, and on each pack is a New Zealand Made
logo.

NEW ZEALAND MADE

36mm rectangle

The 36mm rectangle is an alternative option when the triangle
doesn't suit the visual aesthetic of your brand.

Sound Branding

Floc 3D goes beyond the performance of regular acoustic interior panelling. It does so by weaving New Zealand grown wool into the fabric of their panels.

Floc 3D weaves New Zealand grown wool with superior acoustic design providing a sustainable and locally grown solution for building-interiors around the country.

"It's great to be able to offer an acoustic product that is so intrinsic to New Zealand; grown here, designed here, and made here." – Hedda Oosterhoff, Architectural Manager at T&R Interior Systems

The result is effortless speech that can be heard and ears that don't tire of a tinny echoing timbre. New Zealand's corporate meeting rooms are the home of many Floc 3D panels with demand growing in offices where wellbeing is equally prioritised with productivity.

Photo: T&R Systems

Bigger Is Better

The bigger the product, the bigger the label you'll
need. Steelfort manufacture a number of lawnmowers
including the FineCut SP Instart SP and Metro M&C.

40mm label

Each lawnmower includes the 40mm New Zealand Made label
next to the 4 Year Lawnmaster Warranty label, connecting the
promise with the guarantee.

The lawnmower engine origin is also clearly labelled to
ensure consumers are clear on where both the
engine and the lawnmower body and catcher
are manufactured.

Photo: Steelfort

On The Construction Site

Aquacomb's potable water system pictured has the capacity to hold 10,000 litres of rain water for re-use as drinking water, laundry and other everyday household needs. The pictured installation was completed within five hours without any use of an excavator.

60mm label

The single biggest use of indoor water is the flushing toilet which uses 11 litres of water per flush. A family of four uses around 176 litres a day in the toilet alone. The average washing machine uses around 100 litres of water per wash cycle and a garden hose can spray around 30 litres of water per minute.

By re-using onsite rainwater, you avoid water shortages in summer by accessing your own tanks and avoid the cost of paying for water utilities.

Photo: Aquacomb

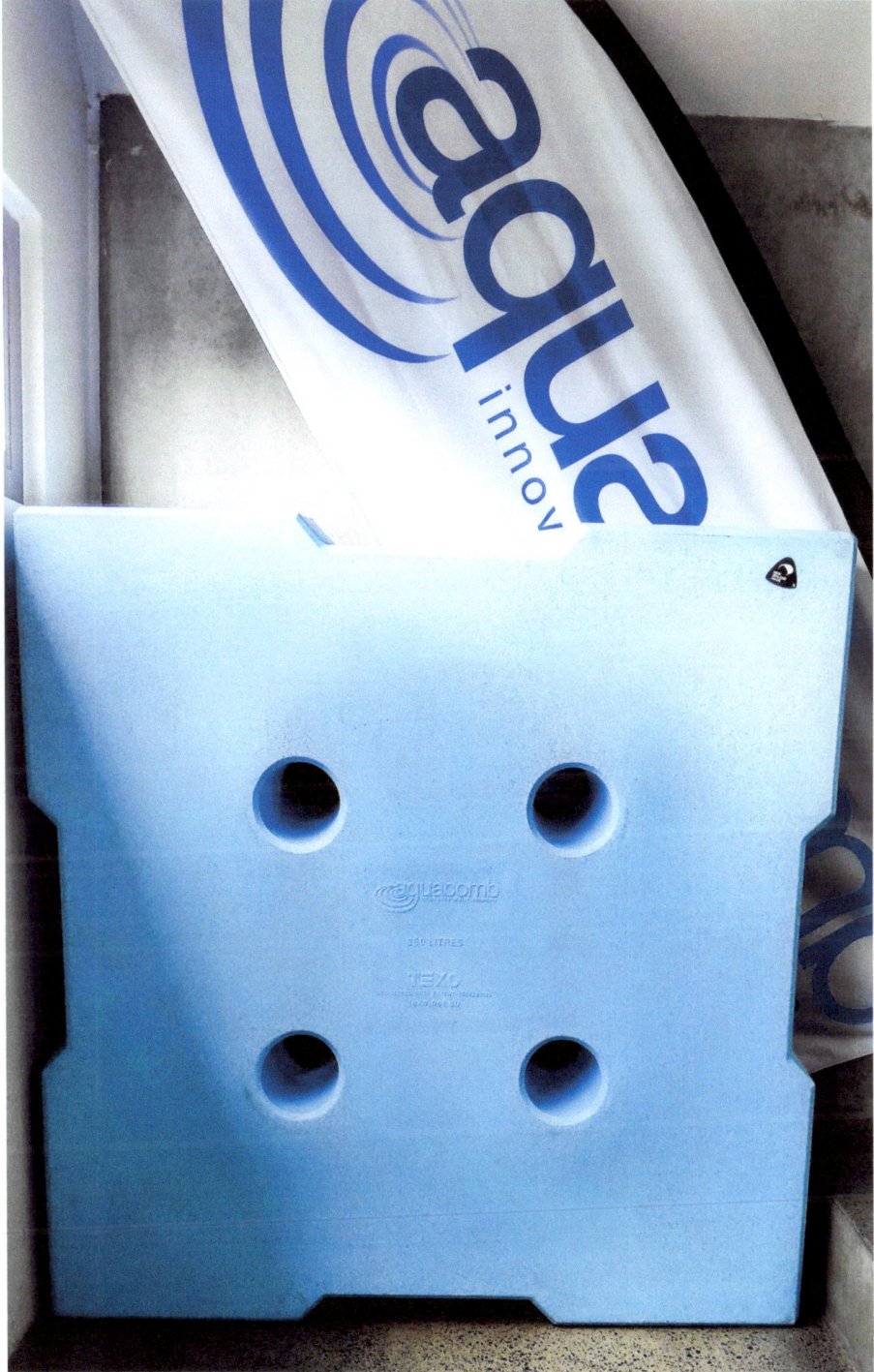

Photo: Aquacomb

Swingtags With Meaning

Chloe Wickman and Sarah Mortimer from Zeenya
Clothing use 50mm swing tags on their clothing lines.
They have a range of leggings and crops that are
designed and made here in New Zealand, all with Kiwi women in
mind.

50mm tag

Knowing who and where their clothing is made is important to
Zeenya. They know who cuts and sews their clothing here in New
Zealand, without labour exploitation.

You'll notice that while the label says New Zealand Made, their
biodegradable fabric is imported from Brazil. That's fine by us
as long as the substantial transformation process of cutting and
sewing the fabric happens here in New Zealand.

Chloe Wickman and Sarah Mortimer   *Photo by: The Style Jungle*

Photo: Zeenya Clothing

New Zealand Made Culture

Contemporary Korowai Designs embraces the gift of Maori culture by helping Kiwis share and celebrate special moments of their lives.

50mm tag

Founder and CEO Brenda Janes makes the Korowai and Kakahu Maori Cloaks given as gifts for welcoming newborns into the world, celebrating birthday milestones such as 21st birthdays as well as marking life's achievements including graduations and weddings and for use at a tangi or unveiling to honour whanau who have passed.

Photo: Contemporary Korowai Designs

"We get amazing comments about the detail and mahi that goes into the korowai and feel proud that our beautiful korowai become a taonga for whānau for generations to come." Brenda Janes, Contemporary Korowai Designs.

Kono is a small Woven basket made from Harakeke which means New Zealand flax. It is used to hold many items and is made by Andrea Taiapa.

Photo: Contemporary Korowai Designs

Tie It In With What You Do

Product branding should say nothing more than it needs to. It's straight forward. It's direct. It displays the Kiwi trademark to tell the audience that this product is New Zealand Made and that is worth something.

50mm tag

It assumes the audience already recognises the Kiwi trademark or values what New Zealand Made means and the brand association helps the consumer with their purchasing decision.

The Kiwi trademark is usually found on the front of the product, near the price tag or in a place likely to be seen while the consumer is evaluating whether this is the one they want.

Tessa at Nuzzle Baby hand makes her products from certified organic cotton and then threads a 50mm swing tag into the rope drawstring.

Photo: Nuzzle Baby

Photo: Lore

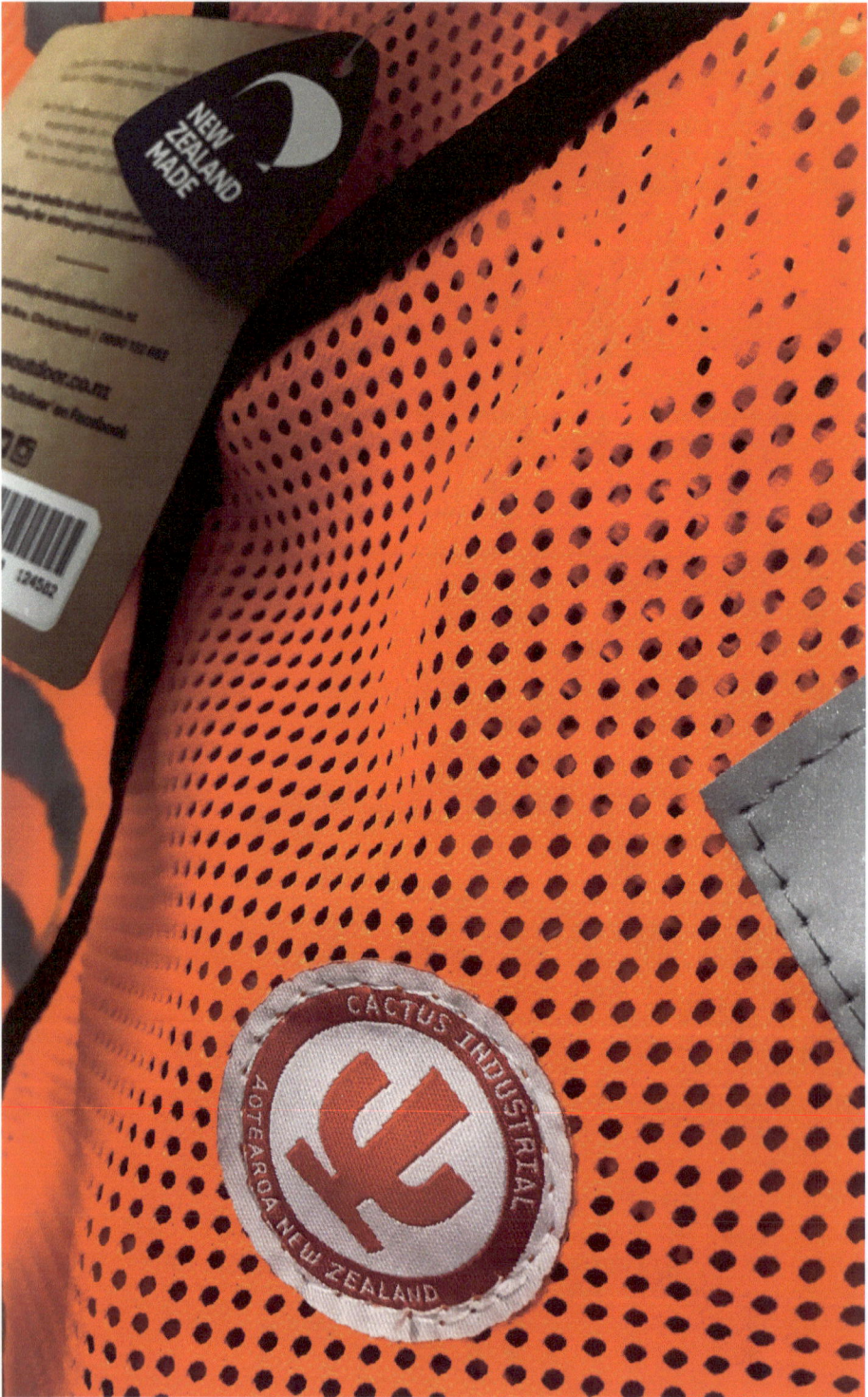

Constructing A Local Future

Cactus Outdoor is synonymous with rugged workwear and packs. There is something of a cult-like status amongst tradies for their durability.

The rise of consumers caring about product provenance combined with the diminishing cost difference of making goods in Asia are two macro trends that has given Cactus Outdoor the confidence to invest.

"We recently purchased Albion Clothing which adds another 80 people to our team and an extra 1750 sqm of manufacturing clout." Ben Kepes, Cactus Outdoor.

The investment speaks to how Cactus Outdoor believes they can build on their 27 year heritage and go further by offering contract manufacturing to other New Zealand brands who want access to their edges of high tech automation and hand-crafted artisan finishing.

Photo: Cactus Outdoor Supertrousers

63

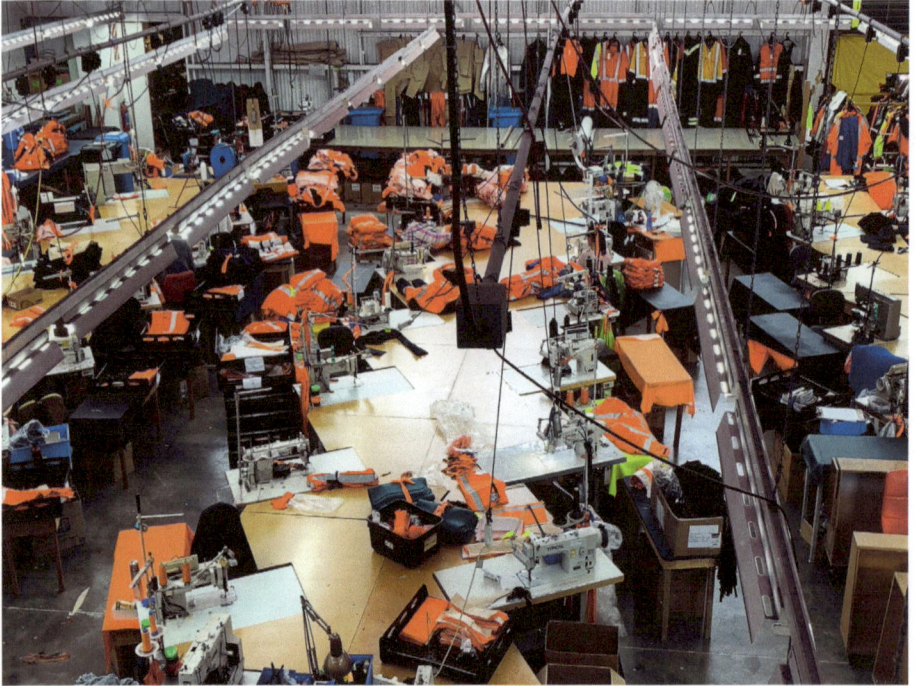

Jaedon Enterprises helps keep New Zealanders safe with workwear Kiwis can trust.

Emergency Response Teams such as the NZ Fire Service, Police, SARS and NZ Coastguard all rely on Jaedon Enterprises for their workwear.

Chainsaw Chaps lowers injury potential when working with chainsaws by covering your legs with fabric that clogs the chainsaw giving you extra precious reaction time.

North End Brewery helped Buy New Zealand Made with a special one-off commemoration beer to celebrate 30 years of the Kiwi trademark.

The Pilsner beer was contract brewed and sent to businesses who have remained with the campaign consecutively for at least 25 years.

CHAPTER TWO

Artwork Applications

We provide you the digital artwork to apply to your products that saves on labelling time.

This chapter looks at various digital artwork solutions for various product and packaging sizes and styles. These fall into five artwork application groups:

Digital
Standard
Inverted
Borderless
Recoloured

AHD

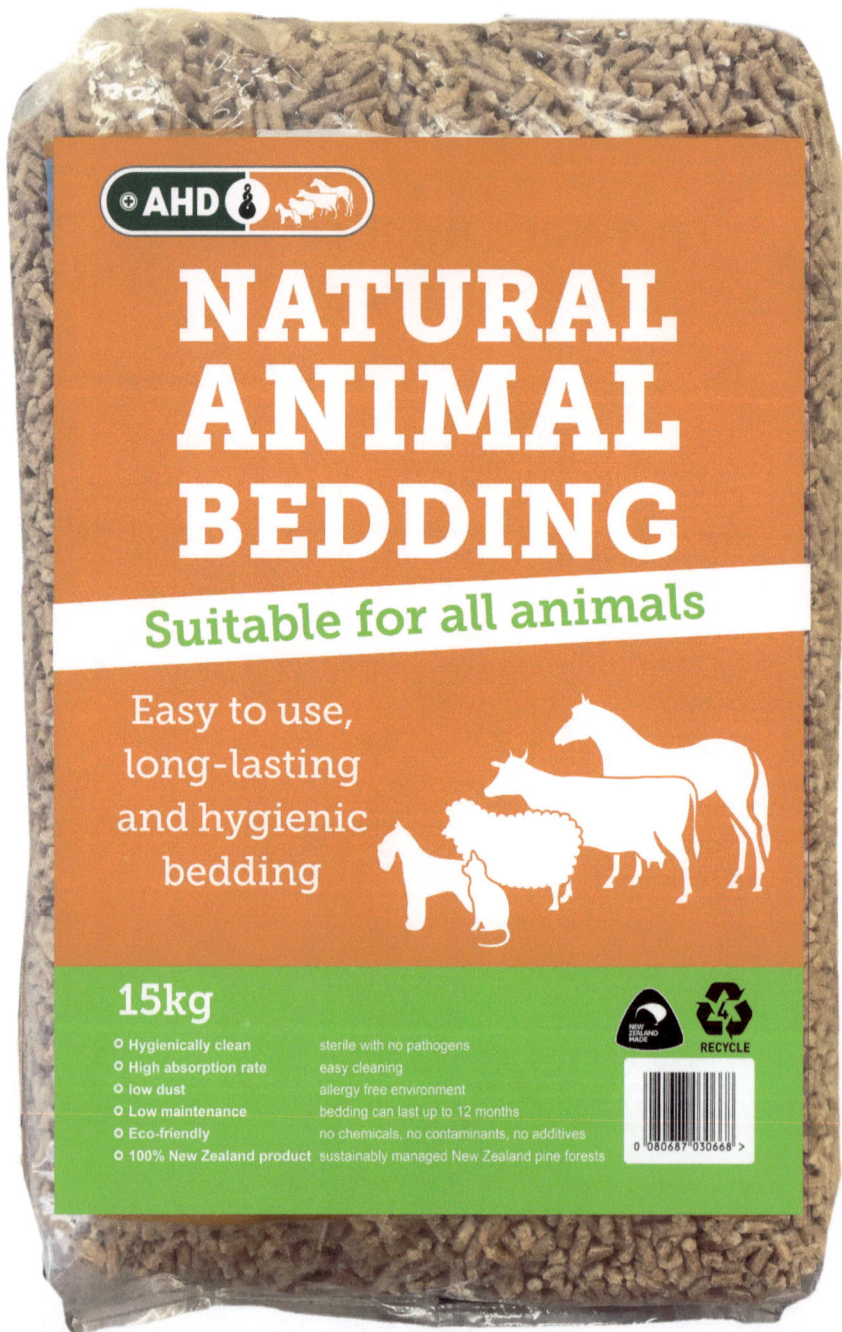

NATURAL ANIMAL BEDDING

Suitable for all animals

Easy to use, long-lasting and hygienic bedding

15kg

Hygienically clean	sterile with no pathogens
High absorption rate	easy cleaning
low dust	allergy free environment
Low maintenance	bedding can last up to 12 months
Eco-friendly	no chemicals, no contaminants, no additives
100% New Zealand product	sustainably managed New Zealand pine forests

NEW ZEALAND MADE

RECYCLE

0 080687 030668 >

Accredit Your Product

A certification mark on a commercial product indicates the existence of an accepted product standard or regulation and a claim that the manufacturer has verified compliance with those standards or regulations.

digital artwork

The Kiwi trademark validates the claim of 'New Zealand Made' in a way that is recognisable with consumers. It is a shorthand way to communicate that what you're offering to the market has been reviewed for eligibility on attributes that buyers value.

When the Kiwi trademark is displayed on a product, it means that a business has been successful in making an application to the Buy New Zealand Made Campaign for a Certificate of Licence. This means that they have provided information about how and where their product is made and what the essential character of that product is.

"It's the assurance that the product is New Zealand made and the company is a New Zealand company that matters to our customers." Richard Kettle, Animal Health Direct.

Certification Location

Where a certification branding approach is taken, the Kiwi trademark is often found on the rear of the product, sometimes alongside other certification marks that make claims about sustainability, safety, durability, popularity and so on. Educated consumers know how to read the labels and will filter out products that don't meet their certification criteria.

The black and white logo is the primary recommended branding option for product certification branding. Stickers or artwork are available that be applied to the rear or side of a product as certification branding as shown opposite and below.

Photo: Nature's Beauty

CONSUMER ENQ

NZ ☎ 0800 730 1

www.bluebird.co.nz

BLUEBIRD FOODS LIMITE
124 WIRI STATION ROAD
MANUKAU, AUCKLAND 2104

Made with care in New Zealand
from local and imported ingredients.

This package is sold by weight not volume;
the settling of contents may occur during transit.

Registered Trademark of the Pepsico Group of
companies. Used in New Zealand Under Licence.

PDPC56216

Display Green Credentials

Health Pak proudly adds the New Zealand Made logo
to hundreds of millions of products seen in cafes and
hotels in New Zealand and around the world. For
many of the 3.8 million visitors who come to Aotearoa every year,
their first New Zealand Made product is likely to be a Health Pak
product, be it a sugar sachet, soap bar, bowl of cereal or shampoo.

Health Pak's latest innovation to
eliminate single-use plastics
from hotels is the worlds
first, paper-based,
Ecostick.

Designed to break down in
landfill in under ten years.
Not only will it fully degrade
in a short space of time, it
represents a 95% reduction in
packaging compared to a
traditional bottle or tube.

Every Ecostick proudly wears
the New Zealand Made logo to
remind the world that it was
designed, developed and made
right here in God's Own.

The logo has been integrated into their packaging as HealthPak
produces hundreds of millions of recylable, paper-based packets
with the New Zealand Made logo every year.

Helping Supermarket Shoppers

Wilson Consumer Products add the Kiwi tradmark across a
number of the brands they manage including King
Soup Mix and Pop'n'Good Popcorn.

"Kiwis want to know the origin of what they're eating and New Zealand Made tells them at a glance." Susan Harvey - Marketing & Business Development Manager.

Artwork Overlays

The modern black and white Kiwi trademark is the primary recommended branding option.

digital artwork

Stickers available in 10mm tiny, 25mm regular, 40mm large and 60mm extra large.

Swing tags available in 50mm size.

Faye Nicoll at Herbology prints the logo directly onto the product packaging.

"It is important to have the logo to inform the public this is a quality product manufactured in New Zealand." Faye Nicoll, Herbology.

Photo: Herbology

Personalised Making Process

When you know the individual name of the person who makes your product, you can use that in your provenance marketing.

For your customers, it personalises the buying experience and helps create a little connection between your business and your customer.

Sunshine Pegs tells the story of Brian, who has been making pegs for the company from the early 1980's.

The story weaves in how their product has been adapted by the seafood industry, vineyards and farms throughout New Zealand to show that New Zealand Made pegs are as relevant as ever nearly 40 years later.

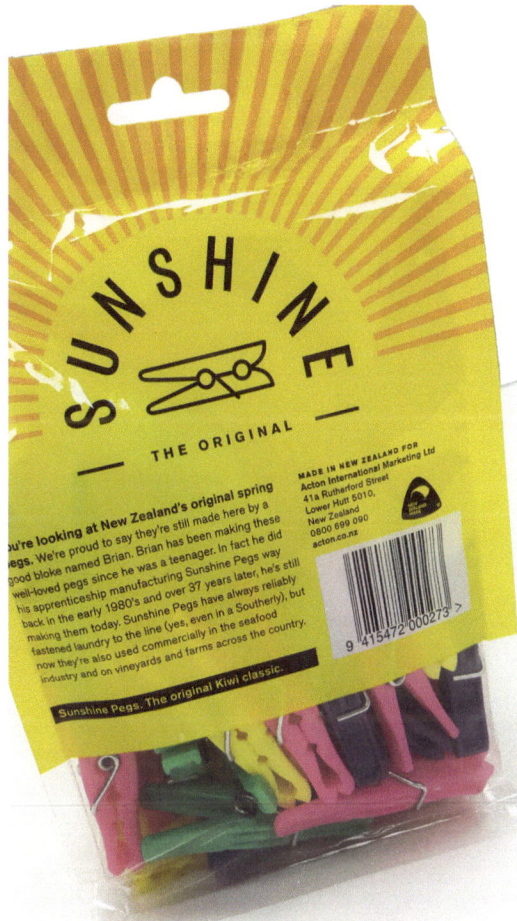

digital artwork

Photo: Sunshine Pegs

77

Photo: The Crafty Chook

Photo: The Crafty Chook

Naming Your Origins

Highlight where in New Zealand you make your product and create a story from that. That is what defines The Crafty Chook range of products by Andrea Rogers.

"The Wild Child Scrub Bars were a no-brainer as we are living on the Wild West Coast and we are all the Children of Mother Nature.

"The names of each soap or scrub bars, are all after people I know or local places. Good Bastard is my Father in Law, Wild Outdoorsman my other half and Gutsy Girl a combo of girls pushing boundaries.

"The benefits of using NZ made for us is instant recognition that we are NZ made and the localisation of products. We believe those are big selling points. The NZ Made is on the front of our products for that instant recognition for the buyer, without having to search the fine print on the back." Andrea Rogers, The Crafty Chook.

Photo: The Crafty Chook

Less Is More

inverted
artwork

The logo can be inverted which is useful where your primary company branding should take visual precedence over the provenance marketing labelling.

On the Shenley Station Blue cheese, Tamin Wilson from Whitestone Cheese Co. displays logos on the front that helps consumers choose. The prominence of their branding is the most obvious along with their product name at the top right.

"Consumers want to know where their food comes from and the New Zealand Made logo helps us stand-out as a local producer amongst the influx of imported cheese hitting supermarket shelves." Tamin Wilson, Whitestone Cheese Co. Marketing Manager.

Photo: Whitestone Cheese Co.

Photo: Honeywrap

Photo: CTS Fishing.

MAVEN

NEW, YET NOSTALGIC, BEAUTIFULLY UNIQUE

Aotearoa Made

Maven's signature crest is an expression of our love f
waterways, and for New Zealand made treasur
New Zealand Made™ Kiwi trademark of

With two harbours, endle
which a multitud

y your Maven ro   ultimate

MAVEN

and push
enjoyment.   to perfection.

NEW ZEALAND MADE™

14

Go Borderless With The White Logo

The logo is available without the triangle in white for use on backgrounds. Oku New Zealand Native Herbal Products have integrated the borderless white logo onto their range of kawakawa tea products.

Grip-Lock is a patented product sold by Aerofast Tiedowns that reduces motorcycle theft through a convenient handlebar lock. The white logo with no triangle is only available as artwork to be applied to a product or packaging, not as a label.

Borderless Kiwi trademark on product

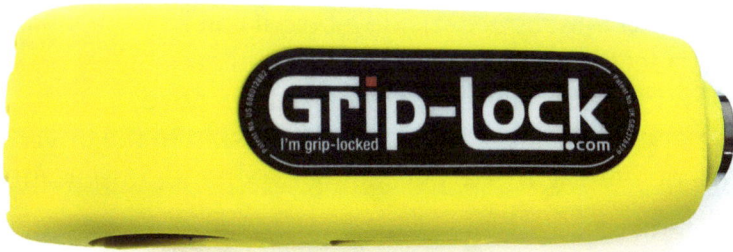

Borderless Kiwi trademark on packaging

Perfection In Packaging

When a product is wrapped inside a box, it can be hard to get a feel for whether you want to buy it. Classic New Zealand solves this through a bespoke packaging approach that presents the sheepskin to the buyer whilst also delivering a luxe packaging experience important to those luxury goods buyers.

"We feature the NZ made logo on most of our packaging or use the swing tags when it is more appropriate. The logo is a mark of trust because it tells buyers that the product is made right here in New Zealand." Kieran Callaghan - Sales Manager, Classic New Zealand.

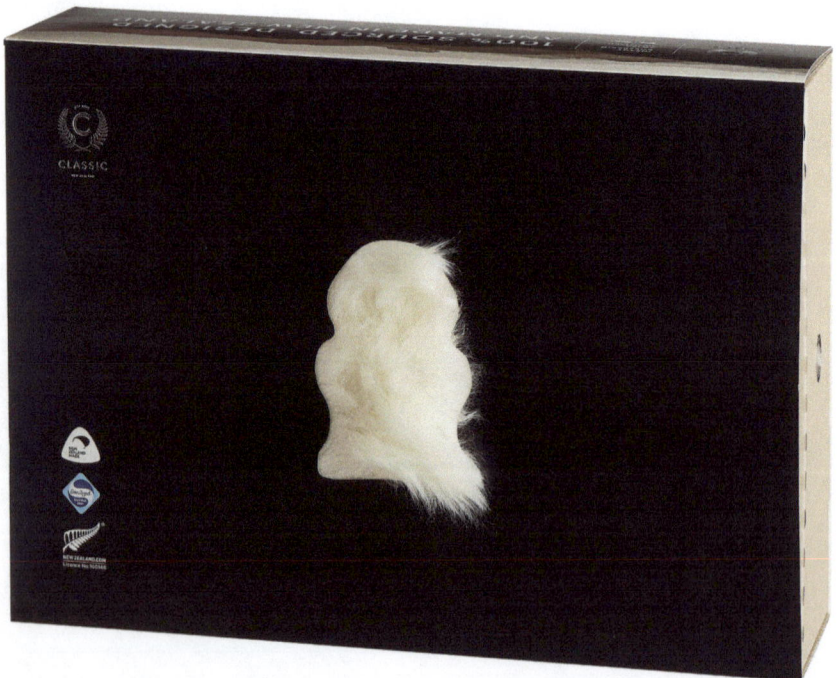

inverted artwork

Photo: Classic New Zealand

Photo: Classic New Zealand

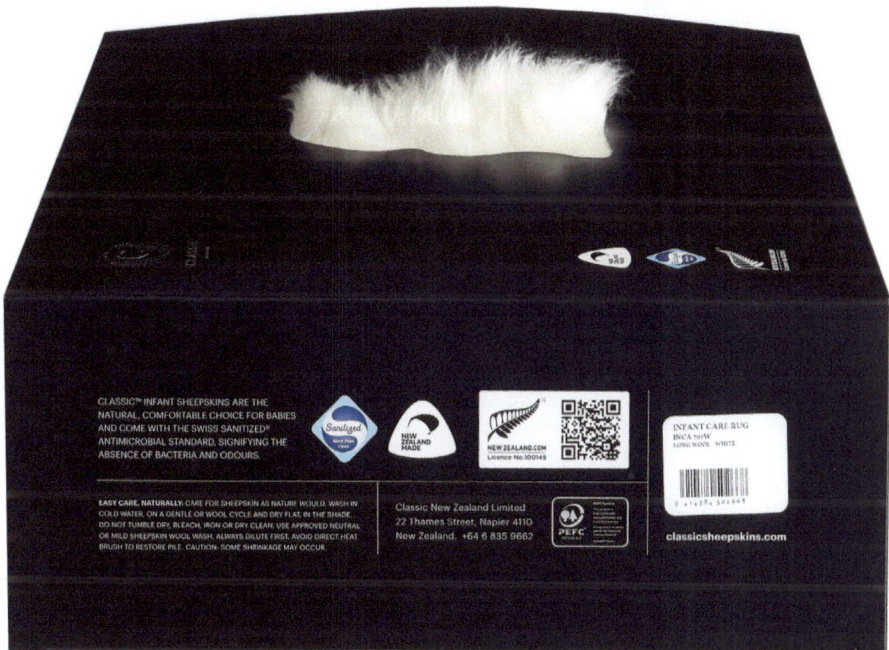

Photo: Classic New Zealand

Eco-Friendly Solid Success

Ethique is helping consumers all over the world 'give up the bottle' and remove single-use plastic from their lives. Their plastic free solid products are all made in New Zealand and cover hair, face, body, baby, household and pet categories.

"Only 9% of plastic worldwide has ever been recycled and annually, 8 million tonnes of plastic ends up in the ocean due to wash off from landfill and improper disposal. To date, we've helped consumers in over 14 countries around the globe collectively save 4.4 million plastic bottles from being made and disposed of in landfills." Brianne West, Ethique Founder & CEO.

Consumers purchase Ethique in over 2,500 stores and e-commerce retailers (including Amazon) across the U.S, New Zealand, Australia, Asia and Europe.

"Our next goal is to save 50 million plastic bottles from going in to landfill by the end of 2025." Brianne West, Ethique Founder & CEO.

Photo: Ethique

Photo: Ethique

Trade Recognition On The Shelf

For over 50 years, the Feltonmix shower mixing valve has been a New Zealand made product with the iconic Kiwi trademark placed proudly on the front side on all Feltonmix packaging.

inverted
artwork

The product is displayed across all trade plumbing merchant stores where the logo can be seen and recognised on the shelves.

Photo: Felton

Adding Product Credibility

For Bronwyn Roberts, Sales & Marketing Director at Odorex® the New Zealand Made logo adds credibility to their range of non-toxic, biodegradable deodorising products.

Each certification logo is presented in white to give the bottle a uniform look while promoting credibility through all of the credentials of the product such as being cruelty-free, recyclable and a long-serving business with 30 years in the trade.

Photo: Odorex

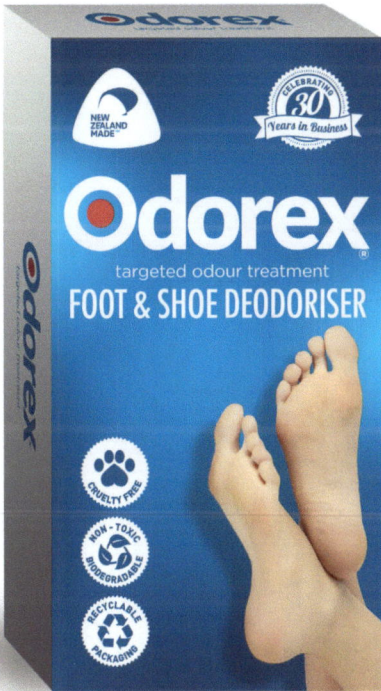

Photo: Odorex

Recoloured Art To Match

Adapt the colour of the logo to suit your branding as long as the Kiwi and the 'New Zealand Made' device are preserved.

recoloured
artwork

Savvy Touch have adapted the background colour of the New Zealand Made logo from black to orange to be in keeping with the colour scheme across their range of products. Each product is represented by a different primary colour.

By recolouring the artwork and maintaining the integrity of the Kiwi trademark, the logo blends in instead of standing out.

Tone It In With What You Make

Snugbags Founder Kim Snel wanted the New Zealand Made logo to both tone in and stand out within her own branding. The teal accent colour highlights the babywear and the 'Merino For Kids' tagline was extended to the logo for this purpose.

"Our customers love that our products are made in New Zealand because they can trust our tailoring to be far superior and our attention to detail to be second to none. Since our fabrics are also made in New Zealand, customers say they can feel the quality difference at first touch – they are so much softer and of higher quality than anything else available." Kim Snel, Snugbags.

Photo: Snugbags

Earth Sea Sky

CHAPTER THREE

Custom Applications

The Kiwi trademark must include the text 'New Zealand Made' except in specific circumstances that must be approved by the Buy New Zealand Made Campaign.

Vehicle signage doesn't need special approval. You can provide the New Zealand Made Kiwi trademark to your vehicle signwriter and they'll do the rest.

Building signage using the New Zealand Made Kiwi trademark must be approved however.

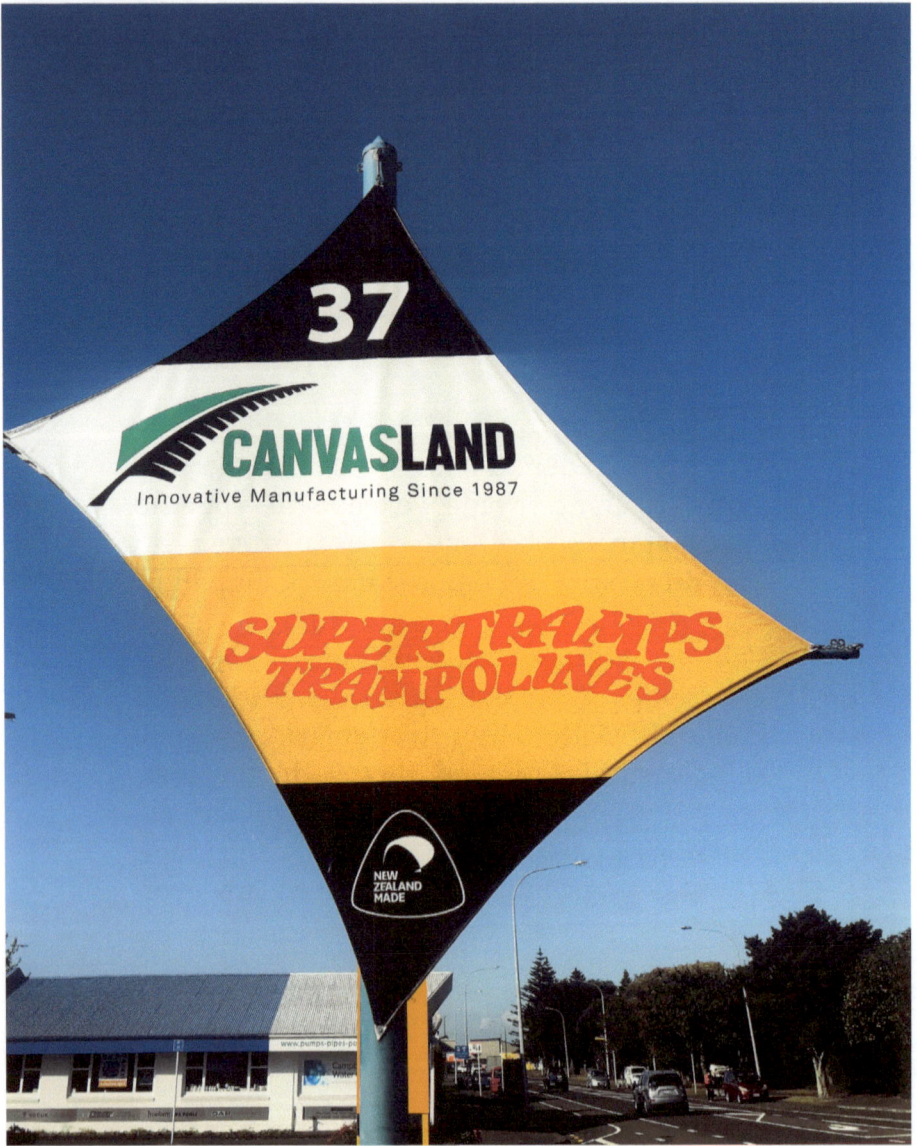

Canvasland has transformed into a diverse company who manufactures product lines across a number of industries including forestry, sporting, agricultural, boating and kayaking.

Canvasland is commissioned on a regular basis to design bespoke and high profile inflatable structures, artistic pieces installed across the Tasman and is home to Supertramp Trampolines –the only brand of trampoline still manufactured in NZ

Building Signage

Signage branding takes the Kiwi trademark and applies it to your building. It makes the most of your real estate to tell everyone that this is your home of manufacturing.

"You've got to support local manufacturing. The money gets returned to workers. It gets returned by an increase in employment and in increase in opportunities. More jobs, more product, more trust and more integrity. Not just our jobs it's the delivery jobs it's the supermarkets, it's the putting it on the shelves, it's the ingredient suppliers, it's everyone.

The jobs stay in New Zealand and the money gets invested back into the business. It doesn't go offshore. It stays here. That's what it's all about." Brent Baillie, Rainbow Confectionery.

Photo: Brent Baille, Anna Heyward (NZ Made), Ryan Jennings (NZ Made), Catherine Keep

Seeing The Kiwi In Etched Glass

Embedded branding takes the essence of the Kiwi trademark and etches it into the product making a physical mark on the product. It is the most integrated way of inter-twining the expectations of your product with the story consumers tell themselves about what New Zealand Made means.

In this format, the Kiwi trademark isn't a tag or a sticker and may not adhere to the modern black and white or classic red and blue colour palette. It probably won't adhere to the standard 25mm size because it's meant to stand out...or be almost completely hidden.

Shown: The Kiwi trademark is etched into lens by Independent Lens Specialist

Embedded branding says to the consumer that being New Zealand Made is right at the heart of what the business does. It has a permanence that communicates 'we can't separate what we make from where we make it.'

Independent Lens Specialists have permission from Buy New Zealand Made to laser etch the Kiwi on its own, into every pair of glasses they manufacture lenses for. If you get your lens prescription from an independent optometrist in New Zealand, next time have a very close look and you might see the iconic New Zealand Made Kiwi right by the frame hinge.

Artwork You'll Need

Start with the Kiwi trademark design and then vary the size to work for what you want the branding to communicate. You may also use any colour or colour combination in relation to the elements of the Kiwi trademark.

The relative proportions of the Kiwi, the New Zealand Made text and the triangle are fixed. Anything outside of this must be approved by the Buy New Zealand Made Campaign.

Vehicle Signwriting

Vehicle creates multiple moving billboards for every vehicle in your fleet. By adding the Kiwi trademark to the front, back or side panels, your business benefits from the instant recognition the logo has with New Zealanders out on the road.

Camco Industries manufacture specialist fitouts that create time efficiencies for tradespeople in construction, field servicing,

infrastructure and power. They're also making sure Kiwis stay safe on the job with fitouts that maximise vehicle payload and simplify loading and unloading to limit operator risk of injury.

"We're keeping thousands of Kiwis safe at work while on the road. Products like our Certified Wellside Cargo Barrier prevent unsecured loads turning into projectiles in the event of an accident. They're a must." Carl Blackman, Camco Industries.

CHAPTER FOUR

Classic Logo Applications

The classic blue and red logo is our longest serving brand that you'll still find on products for our original licence holders from 20+ years ago.

More recently, the classic logo has been adopted by exporters for food and health products to increase buyer confidence in Asia.

Classic Kiwi Export Quality

25mm label

The classic blue and red triangle logo is an evolution of the original logo launched in 1988. It is also a popular choice on products that evoke nostalgia for New Zealand's history.

This logo is also a popular choice in the food and beverage categories, particularly where the product is destined for export to Asia as shown in this example by New Zealand Fish Processing Ltd.

This is the secondary branding option available to the primary black and white logo.

Stickers available in 25mm regular, 40mm large and 60mm extra large.

Swing tags are also available in 50mm size.

Photo: New Zealand Fish Processing Ltd

Photo: New Zealand Fish Processing Ltd

Photo: Maxim by Fielden Metalworks

Gripping Kiwi Ingenuity

NEW ZEALAND MADE

36mm
rectangle

Carac Group is a company known for its innovation in manufacturing engineering. The TrackGrip product attaches to excavators and other tracked vehicles to increase stability, traction and safety particularly in hard to access or steep terrain.

The Standard Grip is perfect for farm track work and light contracting. The Mighty Grip adds additional gussets for excellent sideways protection and the Ultimate Grip is made from a higher grade of steel that makes it harder and better suited to extreme conditions.

Now production is ramping up to supply the demand caused by gaining the attention of a large USA equipment manufacturer.

Photo: Carac Group

"Exporting our products is bringing more jobs to regional New Zealand. That's something I'm personally very proud of." John Burling, Carac Group, Managing Director.

Photo: Carac Group

Love The Outdoors

Founder and Managing Director Gareth Hargreaves
adds the 40mm classic Kiwi logo as a sticker,
underneath his Weapons of Mass Creation logo on the
mountain bike trail crafting tool he makes.

40mm label

The classic blue & red label appeals to Gareth for its 'retro' look and feel that appeals to Kiwis who enjoy getting out and about in our native backyard.

"It ties in with our customers' No.8 Kiwi mentality, ruggedness and no nonsense approach to getting s**t done without the frills." says Gareth Hargreaves.

Photo: WMC Trail Tools

Pearson Engineering. Photo: Trina Snow

Pearson Engineering. Photo: Trina Snow

Kiwi On The Inside

Industrial Automation firm John Brooks labels the inside of electronic boxes they programme to create a visible mark of the intelligent code combined with manufacturing they are building.

60mm label

John Brooks creates their own milk and vacuum pump controller products for supply to the New Zealand and international dairy industry.

John Brooks Automation. Photo: Trina Snow

Immediately Obvious Origin

The front of the label makes it immediately obvious to shoppers that the provenance of your product is New Zealand.

Okau Valley labels their multi-flora mānuka honey with the Kiwi trademark right on the front of the jar.

Photo: Okau Valley

Two Certifications Is Better Than One

NZ Gold Health combines both the New Zealand Made Kiwi trademark and the UMF Honey quality trademark on their products.

This combination assures consumers that they can trust the source of their mānuka honey in the forest of the Haupiri Lake on the west coast of New Zealand.

Photo: NZ Gold Health

Make New Zealand Paradise

The classic Kiwi trademark looks great on the front of industrial-strength products when you want to influence a purchaser who rates the effectiveness of a New Zealand manufactured product as higher than the imported equivalent.

Pest Off! is more effective at a lower active ingredient dose than imports and is one of a range of pest control tools produced by Orillion.

This will likely accelerate New Zealand's goal of being 'predator-free' by 2050 by protecting vulnerable native species, aid with sustainable farming and protect New Zealand's beef, dairy and venison exports.

Photo: Orillion

50mm tags also available. Photo: Trina Snow

Talula Tween Wear finish their giftwrapping with the NZ Made logo and the Talula logo.

Founder Ingrid Gordon is the voice of fashion for 8 - 14 year old girls in New Zealand.

CHAPTER FIVE

Exclusive Logo Applications

The New Zealand Grown logo is exclusively for use on products where all the raw ingredients are 100% grown in New Zealand.

This chapter looks at the ways of applying the Kiwi trademark to what you grow and produce for compliance with the Country of Original Food Labelling Act.

We also look at the application of the exclusive hologram label and the imprint fashion label.

Harry Van Lier, Co-Owner Van Lier Nurseries   Photo: Van Lier Nurseries

New Zealand Grown

The New Zealand Grown logo is exclusively for use on products where all the raw ingredients are 100% grown in New Zealand.

Van Lier Nurseries prominently display the New Zealand Grown logo on their new 100% recyclable paper sleeves for their premium roses, standard roses and complementary flower products.

The packaging has been sourced from a supplier who relies on a sustainable tree replanting program and the ink is natural, making their packaging 100% recyclable.

"It is important for our customers to know that their flowers are of the freshest quality, grown using sustainable practices and don't contain poisonous contaminants used on flower stems overseas." Joanne Hurley, General Manager, Van Lier Nurseries.

Photo: Helius Therapeutics

Photo: Helius Therapeutics

The Grass Is Greener

Helius Therapeutics is leading the trend for an entirely new industry, growing medicinal cannabis to service a $200 billion global marketplace.

"When it comes to natural health and food products, we know that New Zealand provenance gives us an edge. We see enormous potential for exporting New Zealand Grown cannabis products to the world." Paul Manning, Helius Executive Director.

The New Zealand Grown label is being applied across their range including including capsules, sublingual drops, vaporisers and transdermal medicines, containing cannabinoids like CBD and THC, created in their world-class research centre.

When the Buy New Zealand Made Campaign began 30 years ago, it would have been difficult to foresee the change in attitudes that has made licencing of this product category possible.

Photo: Helius Therapeutics

HOW TO CREATE THE WORLD'S PUREST TEA

Nurture the finest tea plants in New Zealand's rich, fertile soil. Farm organically, keep this environment free of chemical sprays and fertilisers. Carefully pick and process according to time-honoured traditions and world-leading ISO22000 HACCP food safety standards.

The result is Zealong, a premium award-winning tea with superb aroma and flavour, achieved without compromise.

manufactured under a management system with ISO and HACCP by SGS New Zealand.

ZEALAND

Naturally Grown Insecticide

The agricultural sector needs bees to survive, yet they have historically relied on insecticides that include a chemical that is highly toxic to bees. Whether it's grapes to make wine, kiwifruit for export, dairy milk powder or organic farming, we all need bees to survive in New Zealand.

"The problem with many insecticides is they are toxic to bees and remain in the soil for up to ten years after the initial spraying. Any crops planted during that decade will take up the insecticide and incorporate it into their flowers. Any insect that visits the plant including bees will die." Greg Duncan, PyrethrumNZ Founder.

Greg Duncan grows pyrethrum specifically for the purpose of extracting the naturally occurring pyrethrins for use in insect control products.

"I want to be part of the change to stop harmful chemicals being used on New Zealand grown crops. Beyond New Zealand, we can export what we grow amd reverse the damage to our insect population globally."
Greg Duncan, PyrethrumNZ Founder.

The Imprint Label

Our newest addition to the trademark family is the imprint label. A soft white card made from cotton byproduct is debossed and formed into a 35mm label.

Ideal for fashion apparel, this label leaves behind a memorable impression.

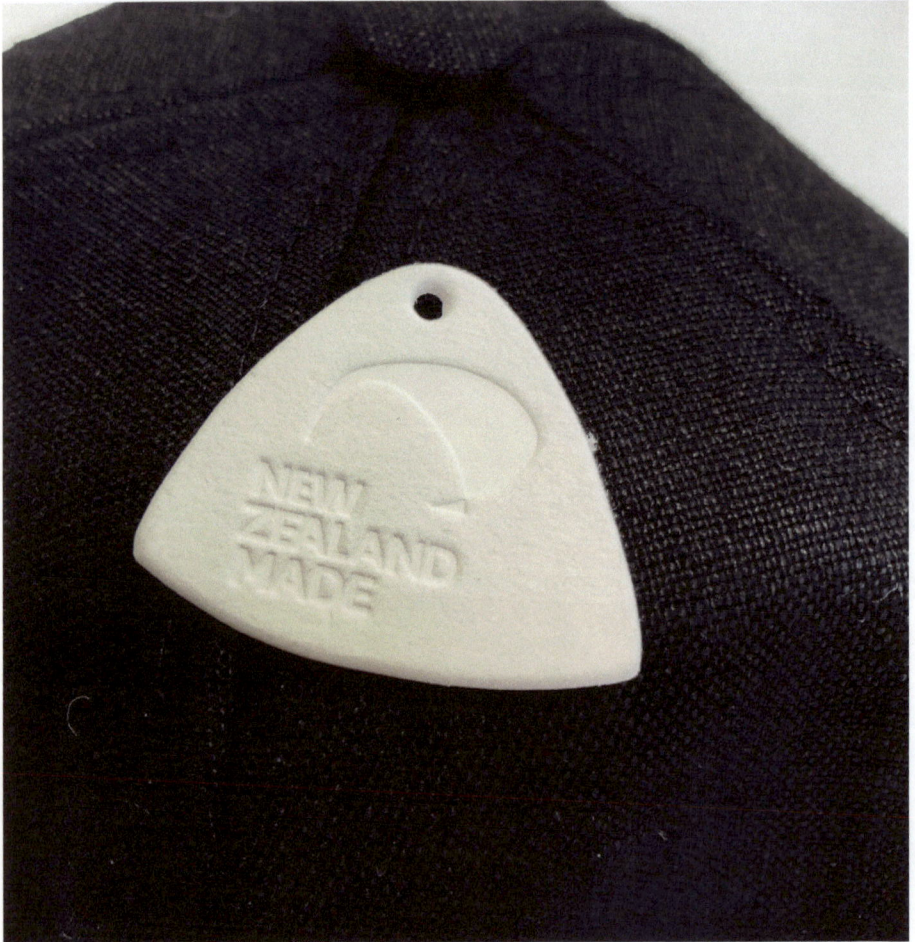

Photo: 35mm Imprint label

The Exclusive Hologram

The hologram attracts attention to your products in a different way. Available in lots of 100, this is one of our newest labelling additions. Ideal to add to your apparel or high end produce such as honey or health products.

Photo: 25mm Hologram label

APPENDIX

Logo History & Uses

The 30 years of the Buy New Zealand Made Campaign has left a visible imprint on the products we have collectively purchased, enjoyed, owned and shared; with each logo representing a moment in time.

This chapter revisits the logos millions of Kiwis have been guided by in their purchasing decisions over the last three decades.

30 Years Of New Zealand Made Artwork

During the 1980's, market shocks affected New Zealand manufacturers as the walls of protection that New Zealand had enjoyed for over 40 years were dismantled. The Kiwi dollar was floated and on its first day rose upwards by 20% and the regulations requiring country of origin labelling on products were repealed.

The Kiwi symbol started appearing on products to demonstrate it was made in New Zealand and there was a lot of sympathy from the public.

"The Kiwi had always been part of the letterhead of the New Zealand Manufacturers Federation. We formed a separate company to do the licensing and enforcement and decided to call it the Buy New Zealand Made Campaign." Barry Brill, inaugural Chairman of Buy New Zealand Made Campaign.

The Kiwi trademark merchandise and branding options released after the initial launch of the Buy New Zealand Made Campaign in 1988.

Kiwis were fearful that jobs would be lost from the influx of cheaply made goods and there was national pride and loyalty in buying products made in New Zealand.

Initially the campaign was to run for six months, yet over the last 30 years it has become a highly regarded symbol domestically and in our most important export markets.

The artwork has evolved over this period, both in its design and its meaning. Buying New Zealand Made initially meant 'keep your country working. That phrase was dropped in the early 1990's and replaced with a 'Buy NZ Made' and a "New Zealand Made' option from then on. The iconic Kiwi has remained central throughout all iterations of the logo since.

The evolution of the New Zealand Made logo, from 1988 through to 2012 that have been replaced by the current Kiwi trademark.

Work of art by Michael Stevenson; artist; 2003-2005; New Zealand.
Displayed at Wellington City Museum 2018.

The Škoda powered Trekka was a light utility vehicle manufactured in New Zealand between 1966 and 1973. It is the only vehicle designed and manufactured in New Zealand to have entered commercial production for an extended period.

Avoid Incorrect Logo Use

Incorrect logo use of the Kiwi trademark can be costly to fix for a business and can reflect negatively on your brand. Please ensure you stick to the guide and avoid the following branding mistakes:

1. Do not incorporate the Kiwi trademark into your own logo.

2. Do not swap the 'triangle device' for a circle.

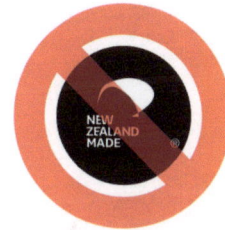

3. Do not remove the words 'New Zealand Made'.

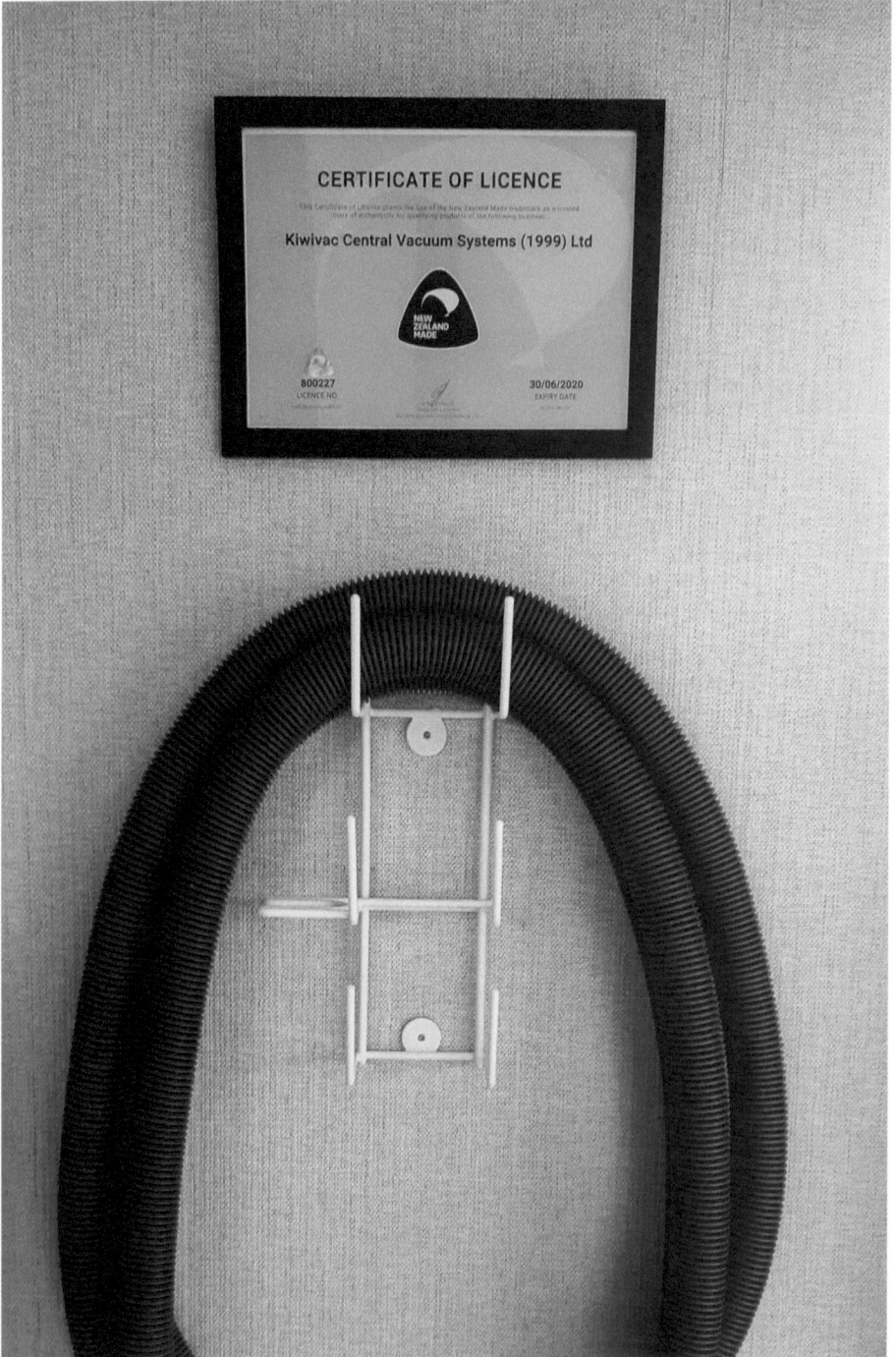

Photo: *Kiwivac Central displaying their Certificate of Licence with the 25 years of continuous licence displayed in the top right hand corner*

Fly The Flag For New Zealand Made

Tap in to the built up trust of the iconic Kiwi trademark by flying the flag at your next event, tradeshow or in-store promotion. Of course the New Zealand Made flag can be flown from a flagpole too next to the New Zealand flag if your headquarters has the facilities.

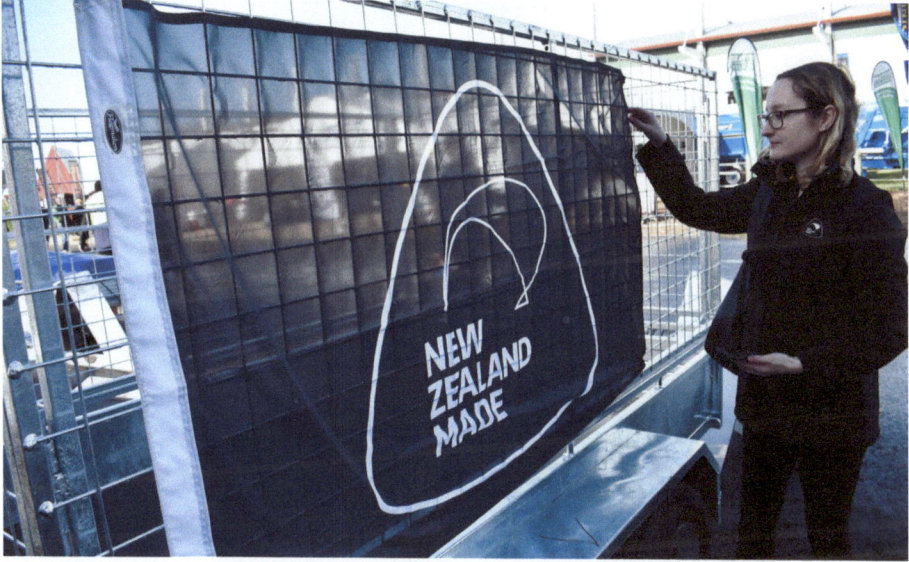

Pictured: Anna Heyward putting the final touches on Pinto Trailers at Fieldays

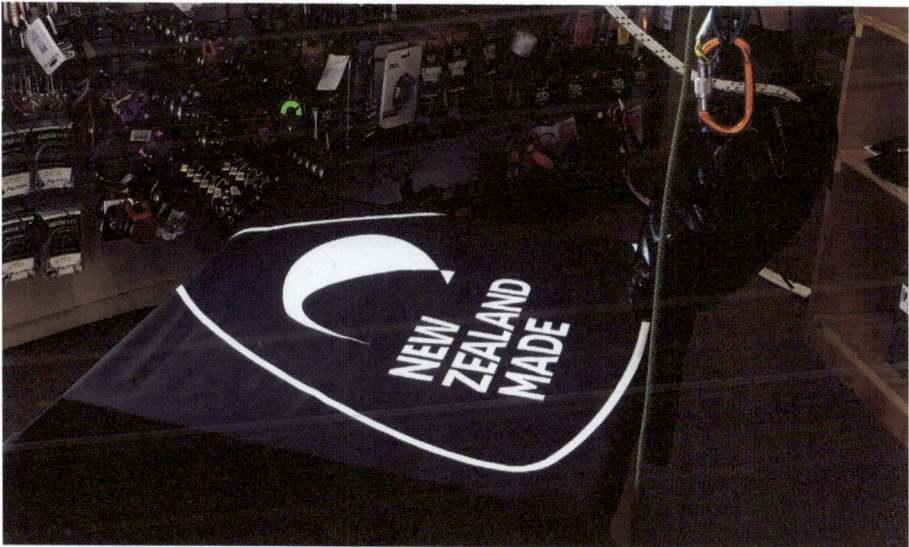

Aspiring Safety fly the New Zealand Made flag in their showroom

141

Go Make Your Edge

www.ingramcontent.com/pod-product-compliance
Lightning Source LLC
Chambersburg PA
CBHW040931030426
42334CB00007B/114